THE WORD GOBBLERS

A HANDBOOK FOR PARENTS WORKING WITH CHILDREN STRUGGLING TO READ

CATHERINE MATTHIAS

ILLUSTRATED BY JOAN GILBERT

SQUAREONE™ PUBLISHERS

Cover Designer: Jeannie Rosado
In-House Editor: Erica Shur
Typesetter: Gary A. Rosenberg
Illustrations: Joan Gilbert

The distortion copy found on pages 22 through 37 were reprinted with permission from copyright materials owned by the Perceptual Development Corp. The name Irlen® is a registered trademark owned by the Perceptual Development Corp. and is used by permission.

Square One Publishers
115 Herricks Road
Garden City Park, NY 11040
(516) 535-2010 • (877) 900-BOOK
www.squareonepublishers.com

Library of Congress Cataloging-in-Publication Data
Names: Matthias, Catherine, author.
Title: The word gobblers : a handbook for parents working with children
  struggling to read / Catherine Matthias, Certified Irlen Syndrome
  Screener ; Illustrated by Joan Gilbert.
Identifiers: LCCN 2020042788 | ISBN 9780757005022 (paperback) | ISBN
  9780757055027 (epub)
Subjects: LCSH: Reading (Elementary) | Vision disorders in children. |
  Learning disabled children--Identification. | Parent and child. | Irlen
  syndrome
Classification: LCC LB1573 .M3795 2021 | DDC 372.4--dc23
LC record available at https://lccn.loc.gov/2020042788

Printed in India

10   9   8   7   6   5   4   3   2   1

Contents

To Helen Irlen and the Irlen Institute
for their pioneering work in helping
children and adults with reading difficulties.

Acknowledgments

The production of a book is rarely a solitary endeavor. There are those who have encouraged the writer, perhaps for years. There are those who have been directly involved with a manuscript by being early readers, offering suggestions for the sake of clarity. There are book writing groups and freelance editors, who take a deeper dive into critiquing initial efforts. Then there are the publishers and editors and artists who work to create the best book possible for the intended audience. And if the book is nonfiction, then credit must go to all those who added to the knowledge of a specific field through publication of their research. To all of these people, I owe my thanks.

My profound thanks and respect to Helen Irlen and the Irlen Institute for their deep and continuing research into the ability of the brain to process visual information and for helping children and adults overcome the difficulties they encounter when this process is disrupted. To Marcia Davis, Certified Irlen Diagnostician, who recognized my potential and trained me to become a Certified Irlen Screener. A second thank you to Marcia Davis, and to Fran Renk, Certified Irlen Diagnostician, for reading my early efforts at producing *The Word Gobblers*, and giving me valuable feedback.

Thank you to the Society of Children's Book Writers and Illustrators, both national and local (Oregon) for their work supporting writers and illustrators of children's books. To Writer's Digest for its magazine, website, and conferences helping writers of all genres. To Fishtrap, a local nonprofit, for its support of writers living in the West. To Mark Malatesta, author advocate and mentor, for his support and constant good cheer. To Holly Adler, independent editor, for her valuable critiques and friendship.

To everyone at Square One, but especially Rudy Shur, publisher, for believing in the importance of *The Word Gobblers* and for keeping me on track, my deepest thanks. To In-House Editor, Erica Shur, for giving *The Word Gobblers* a coherent layout, and for being a pleasure to work with throughout the process. To Gary Rosenberg, typesetter extraordinaire, for understanding the special needs of this book. To Jeannie Rosado for her delightful cover design.

My thanks to Joan Gilbert, freelance illustrator and friend, for giving *The Word Gobblers* a colorful life, and for being so much fun to work with.

To my friends, thank you to all the Eagle Cap Scribblers children's book writers: Joan Gilbert, Nancy Lee-Noelle, Jenny Moore, Rebecca Lenahan, Pam Royes, Dawn Highberger, and Kathy Hunter. To Cynthia Hilden, who introduced me to Irlen Syndrome, opening a new world to explore. To Melissa Reardon, Jan Rimerman, Lynn Peterson, Russ Rotzler, Elnora Cameron, Jackie MacGregor for reading my manuscript and asking questions that helped me clarify my presentation. To Rich Wandschneider, founder of Fishtrap, friend and advocate. To Alex Case, Lynn Wolf, Kathleen Ellyn, Tamara Fuchs, Tom Fuchs, David Carpenter, Melissa Duncan, Abby Beauchamp, Kendra Kirkpatrick, Mark Peterson, Katherine Stickroth, and Billie Suto for helping me earn my screener certification by volunteering to be my initial subjects. To Dr. Troy Bailey, Wallowa Valley Eye Care, for his support and advocacy. And to the many who have cheered me on, thank you.

To my mother, Kay Matthias, who was always my most ardent cheerleader. To my cousin and best friend, Eva Cavanaugh Jankowski, who was there from the beginning. To my wonderful children and stepchildren, Dustin Kelly, Lisa Laser, Louisa Jones, and Hillary Dames for their sweet enthusiasm. My grandchildren, Ellis, Nico, Beatrice, Charlie, and Caroline for their never ending curiosity and ability to play, and because grandkids are simply the best. Lastly and mostly, Stewart Jones, my husband and soul mate, for his unconditional support and for laughing in all the right places at all the right times.

Foreword

The Word Gobblers is a captivating book that engages you in discovering a new way of thinking about reading. It provides a method that may change you or your child's relationship to reading so that it becomes efficient, painless, and allows you to read with good comprehension. This book is designed for parents whose children are struggling in school and may not know why or what to do to help them. This book provides parents with the knowledge of what questions to ask, and what to do for these bright children who are struggling to succeed.

Many years ago I became aware that as a school psychologist I was unable to help certain children who were struggling in school. I started a research project with adult students at a local university where I headed the Adults Learning Disability Program. These students blamed themselves for their reading difficulties and were shocked and angry to discover how different reading was for good readers. They wanted me to make their reading skills just like everyone else. I spent many months trying every method designed to improve reading. One day a student brought in a red plastic see-through folder which she placed over a page of printed text. Another student looked over her shoulder and shouted, "Helen, you made me aware that words move when I read. The words, they are not moving with the red plastic sheet!" All the other adult students in the program came over to look, but the red color didn't help them.

We invaded the theater department where each student found a different colored plastic sheet which made the words easy to read improving comprehension, sustained attention, and comfort. The students cried with joy and ran around telling everyone. The news spread like wildfire on campus and other students with reading problems were flocking to my office hoping that one of those colors would work for them. I refined the technique and developed a testing method to identify those students whose reading and other academic activities could be helped with color which is now called the Irlen Method.

The program I have created has come a long way since then. Discovering and refining the Irlen Method was not always a simple journey, in spite of the dramatic results. Research has shown that for many people suffering from various learning disabilities the Irlen Method can make a world of difference. Additionally, the system can also improve other areas beyond reading for those who have this syndrome. Today, the Irlen Institute has certified hundreds of thousands of Irlen Syndrome Screeners and Diagnosticians throughout the world who are out there helping both children and adults improve their learning skills.

This book by Catherine Matthias, an Irlen Screener, is specifically designed for every parent who has ever watched their child struggle to read or could not understand why their child doesn't like to read. I may be a little biased, but honestly, there are so many children and adults who suffer silently, and do not realize that reading can become easy with the Irlen Method described in this book. Catherine has also included exercises to help readers determine if they should take the next step—that is to have their child evaluated by a Certified Irlen Syndrome Screener or Irlen Diagnostician.

Colorful wishes,
Helen L. Irlen, MA, BCPC, PPS, BCPTSD, LMF
Founder & Executive Director of the Irlen Institute
International Headquarters

Preface

Nine-year-old Ben was a beautiful child with chocolate-brown eyes that sparkled with curiosity. Although his vocabulary was advanced for his age, his reading level was a full year behind his grade level. In addition, he'd been diagnosed with attention deficit hyperactivity disorder, commonly referred to as ADHD.

Ben's mother had read an article in the local newspaper about my earning certification as an Irlen Syndrome Screener. The training gave me the tools to evaluate children and adults for the possibility of having this syndrome that causes reading problems due to a processing malfunction within the brain.

It was Ben's grandmother who brought him to see me. She watched as I worked with him through a set of tasks that included questions about his symptoms, observation of his behavior, and systematically finding the colored overlays (plastic sheets placed over white paper) that gave him the greatest relief from his symptoms. During questioning, Ben told me that when he rode in a car, it looked as if the roadside trees were falling in on him. My heart broke as I imagined what it must have been like as a toddler strapped into a car seat to see trees falling toward him.

After working with Ben for over an hour, I found the right combination of colored overlays. I had him read a paragraph out loud using white paper with black ink from a story appropriate to his reading level. His reading was choppy, hesitant, and filled with mistakes. No judgments were made concerning his performance.

Next, I had Ben read a different passage at the same level using two overlays, aqua over purple. His reading became smoother and less hesitant, and he made far fewer mistakes. He looked up at me and smiled. I smiled back, then glanced toward his grandmother. She, too, had heard the difference. Tears ran down her cheeks.

I gave Ben three overlays to take home with him—a purple and two aqua—to use under different lighting conditions. I gave his grandmother the name and contact information for an Irlen Diagnostician who could test Ben for his specific formula for Irlen Spectral Filters (specially tinted plastic lenses worn like eyeglasses). Within a few weeks, Ben was tested and fitted for his lenses, allowing him to enter fourth grade on a more level playing field.

I'd first heard of Irlen Syndrome and the Irlen Institute while having lunch with a friend, a retired college counselor. I was lamenting the difficulties my two oldest grandchildren had with reading in spite of years of remedial help. They were both bright, with vocabularies beyond their years, engaging, and involved with the world around them, but their struggles were having repercussions on all aspects of their lives.

My friend asked if I'd ever heard of Irlen Syndrome. I hadn't. She told me about a student she'd helped by introducing her to colored overlays. That night I stayed up reading the Irlen Institute's website and ordering all the books they offered. I was perplexed. Why hadn't I learned of this sooner? Why wasn't this breakthrough being shouted from the rooftops? In Australia, every school-aged child is tested for Irlen Syndrome. Why wasn't this happening in the US? Why wasn't this happening in every country?

Because I'd already had several children's books published, I started writing a book about Irlen Syndrome aimed at eight- to twelve-year-olds called THE WORD GOBBLERS—*They Munch. They Crunch. They Scrunch.* However, after training to become a Certified Irlen Screener, I realized the audience I wanted to reach was those who live with children who struggle to read: their parents. I kept the title, but changed the focus.

I wanted the book to be an interactive book, with adult and child working together, and simple enough to not be overwhelming. It needed to provide enough information to advance the process from recognizing the problem to recognizing there may be a solution if certain factors are exposed, such as finding out if reading on colored paper eases your child's discomfort. I hope you will find this format useful.

Half of the author's profits from the sale of this book after promotion costs will be donated to the Irlen Syndrome Foundation to support low-income families seeking support for Irlen Syndrome screening and diagnostic services.

Names of clients have been changed or omitted to protect their privacy.

Catherine Matthias
Certified Irlen Screener

Introduction

Is your child reading below grade level? Does your child miss words while reading? Read choppily or hesitantly? Have difficulty staying focused? Complain of headaches or stomachaches when reading? Does your child avoid reading? These are just a few examples of the symptoms that might be displayed if your child has Irlen Syndrome—a malfunction in the brain's ability to process visual information.

Parents are usually the first ones to observe these behaviors or hear their child's complaints. Parents may notice other symptoms long before their child is of school age. These may include being bothered by glare or a preference for dim lighting, mood changes, depth perception problems that show up as clumsiness or poor sports performance, such as not being able to catch a ball.

If any or several of these symptoms are displayed by your child, working though the tasks in this book will help determine if Irlen Syndrome could be the cause. Also discussed are remedies that will ease symptoms and help your child live a more productive and satisfying life.

The title of this book, *The Word Gobblers*, came about because I want children who struggle with reading to understand that just as food or pollen allergies are not their fault, neither is difficulty with reading. Just as important, by using the right tools, children can conquer those nasty Gobbler characters who munch and crunch and scrunch words and numbers.

Although this book is written for parents who are on the front lines when dealing with their child's symptoms and behaviors, it can also be useful to teachers, who occupy an important place in children's lives, and who must accommodate the various and often competing needs of many children in a single classroom.

Discovery of Irlen Syndrome

Early in her career, Helen Irlen became the coordinator of a federally funded adult learning disability program at California State University–Long Beach. Over a two-year period, she interviewed more than 1,500 adults, ranging in age from 18 to the mid-40s. She noticed a sub-group emerging: individuals who had adequate decoding skills and sight vocabulary, and good phonetic skills, but who avoided reading as much as possible because it was so difficult, and the longer they read, the more difficult it became.

What happened next is something Helen Irlen calls a lucky break. I call it paying attention. One of the five students she was working with brought a red colored overlay with her to class. The student had used it for vision training exercises four years earlier. As stated by Helen Irlen in her book, *Reading by the Colors*, "Another student put the colored sheet on the page she was looking at and gave a little scream. It was the first time she had ever been able to read without having the words constantly sway back and forth."

The results of that "lucky break" were years of experiments and studies, the development of an institute dedicated to the study of Irlen Syndrome, the creation of specifically colored overlays, the invention of Irlen Spectral Filters, the publication of several in-depth books, and the helping of hundreds of thousands of people around the world who suffer from the symptoms of this syndrome.

What You Will Find in this Book

Chapter One of *The Word Gobblers* is an examination of Irlen Syndrome: what it is, how it is acquired, and what can be done to overcome it. Chapter Two presents a list of questions concerning symptoms your child may exhibit. You can answer the questions for your child by observing the child's behavior or, if the child is old enough and self-aware enough, your child can be asked directly.

Chapter Three shows examples of how a child with Irlen Syndrome might see words and numbers. Chapter Four presents reading exercises for your child using white paper with black ink, then repeats the exercises using various colored papers.

Because children who struggle with reading may suffer from low self-esteem, and are often bullied, Chapter Five lists questions parents can ask children to help them express their feelings and thoughts about these issues. I try to show children who suffer from this condition that they are not alone and they are not at fault. Chapter Six shows parents the next steps to take if this workbook leads them to believe that Irlen Syndrome could be the cause of their child's difficulties with reading.

How to Use this Book

I recommend you first read through *The Word Gobblers* to become familiar with the material. Read through the questions in Chapter Two a second time and observe your child's behavior in relation to those questions.

If appropriate, invite your child to work through the questionnaire with you. Listen carefully. Sometimes children will tell you something that isn't a direct answer to the question, but was something they became aware of because of the question. Be patient. Children, especially young children, are usually unaware that what is happening to them is different than what is happening to others. For example, they may think everyone is bothered by glare or everyone gets headaches when they read or everyone sees a printed page the same way they do.

I screened an eight-year-old girl whose mother, grandmother, and two older sisters observed the session. After asking the young girl a series of questions to determine her symptoms, her fourteen-year-old sister spoke up, "I can answer yes to nearly all those questions." Because her grades were good, no one in her family knew that she, too, was struggling.

Your child may or may not see distortions on a page, but Chapter Three will show you some of the more common distortions reported by those who suffer with Irlen Syndrome. View these pages with your child and explain that some people who struggle to read see pages that look like these. Your child may recognize a distortion, or a page may be doubly confusing because the words are being distorted twice, once on the page and once in the brain. These are the pages that show Gobblers stretching, squishing, and erasing letters, words and numbers.

As you work through the reading tasks in Chapter Four with your child, make no judgments on performance. There are no right or wrong answers.

What you are looking for is your child's comfort level and proficiency. Do not comment on their proficiency, just note it. Do they tell you it is easier to read on a certain color paper compared to the white paper? Do you hear smoother reading when they do the tasks on a colored page compared to a white page? Do they have any of the physical symptoms described in the questionnaire? If yes, your child's reading difficulties point to Irlen Syndrome as the source.

For a child younger than eight, you may only want to work through the individual letters and numbers, especially if the child has not yet started to learn to read words and sentences. For an older child, you may need to move on to the sentences on the reverse sides of the letters and numbers pages before you can hear the child struggling or before the child can feel a greater comfort level with a particular colored page.

The first time you read through Chapter Five, concerning self-esteem and bullying, you may decide there are other questions you want to add to the discussion with your child. A section for note taking has been added to the end of this chapter. Due to the importance of these issues, especially for those who are behind their peers in reading, you may want to introduce your child to one of the many age appropriate books about bullying that your local library or bookstore can provide.

Finally, Chapter Six shows you the next steps to take if your child appears to have Irlen Syndrome. Website information is included in this chapter. If you are unable for any reason to take the next steps, then make the changes outlined in Chapter One, such as using colored paper for assignments and taking many breaks while reading. This will be essential to easing your child's difficulties with reading.

1

What Is Irlen Syndrome?

Seventy percent of all sensory information enters through the eyes and passes to the brain as light waves to be processed. However, one in six people worldwide has Irlen Syndrome—the inability of the brain to properly process certain colors in these wavelengths.

This malfunction means visual information is not being correctly interpreted. Studies by the Irlen Institute have found that for some people certain wavelengths reach the brain at a slower rate than others, making the building of an accurate picture by the brain impossible. When we look at something, anything, we don't see that thing. Instead, we see light waves bouncing off the object or scene. These light waves enter the eye where they are passed on to the brain to be constructed into a picture. When the picture is not complete, difficulties arise.

Irlen Syndrome falls on a spectrum from mild to severe and can affect reading, writing, math, light and glare sensitivity, depth perception, sensory overload behaviors, and overall health. Children who suffer from this condition often display symptoms that include headaches, stomachaches, restlessness, hyperactivity, sleepiness, dizziness, and uncooperative behaviors.

These difficulties can be eased through the understanding of those around them and through the use of a few simple tools: colored paper and Irlen Colored Overlays (specially formulated thin, plastic sheets laid over white paper), improved lighting conditions, and Irlen Spectral Filters (lenses with highly customized colored filters worn like glasses or contact lenses).

Irlen Syndrome affects girls and boys equally, and although heredity accounts for 50 percent of cases, brain injury, including whiplash, high fevers and viruses can also cause the condition. Due to its prevalence (approximately 14 percent of the world's population), Australia utilizes the services of trained and Certified Irlen Syndrome Screeners to evaluate all school aged children for the condition.

Although vision always needs to be checked first when a child suffers with reading difficulties, Irlen Syndrome is not a vision problem. It is a perception problem. Additionally, it is not a learning disability, although it can contribute to difficulties learning.

DYSLEXIA AND IRLEN SYNDROME

Irlen Syndrome may not be the only reason your child struggles to read, but it could be a piece of the puzzle. For example, if your child has been diagnosed with dyslexia, it would also be helpful to have that child screened for Irlen Syndrome. The Irlen Institute reports that one-third of children diagnosed with dyslexia, do not have dyslexia, they have only Irlen Syndrome. Once that is compensated for through the use of colored overlays or Spectral Filters, the child often catches up to grade level within months, while physical symptoms disappear or lessen considerably.

Another third of children diagnosed with dyslexia have both dyslexia and Irlen Syndrome. Unless the light wave processing problem is treated first, remedial steps used to overcome dyslexia will not be effective. If your child still struggles with reading, writing, or math after months or years of remedial intervention and specialized teaching methods, a screening for Irlen Syndrome could be beneficial.

Within one to two hours, a screener can determine if your child is likely to have the condition, what color wavelengths are not being processed properly, and if there are any distortions occurring with letters, numbers, or symbols. You will leave the screening session with colored overlays to help stop the distortions on white paper and ease symptoms of discomfort, such as headaches, stomachaches, and dizziness.

You may also decide to have your child tested for Spectral Filters. It is paramount that you go to a qualified Irlen Diagnostician. The number of color combinations is nearly unlimited. Which colors are needed and in what order the colors are placed makes the difference between success and failure.

IRLEN SPECTRAL FILTERS

A word of caution: It is vital that you do not buy frames with colored lenses, such as pink or yellow sunglasses, to match the color of the Irlen overlay your child finds most comfortable. Irlen Spectral Filters are never the same color as the overlay. Using the wrong colored sunglasses could make your child's symptoms worse. The reason for this is that colored overlays change only the white background of a page or computer screen, making the black letters and numbers easier to read. The overlays do not change the processing problem within the brain.

The advantage of Spectral Filters is they do not change the background color of things such as white paper, clouds, or snow, although they will cut down on glare, a much wanted outcome. Irlen Spectral Filters are able to alleviate distressing symptoms by changing the timing that wavelengths of light reach the brain. This allows the brain to accurately and comfortably process visual information and build a correct picture.

Although Spectral Filters might look like sunglasses, the lenses do not change the color of objects like sunglasses and colored overlays do—white remains white, blue remains blue, and so on. And they do not make the world dark like sunglasses do. What Spectral Filters change is the brain's ability to process information, reducing reading difficulties, distortions, and the stress-caused symptoms of the condition.

IMMEDIATE RELIEF

There are several things parents can do immediately to relieve some of the stress for children with Irlen Syndrome. First, modify lighting situations. Those with the condition are often sensitive to bright light, especially fluorescent light. At home, change to color-balanced light bulbs wherever possible, especially where children do homework.

Color correcting lightbulbs have a color rendering index (CRI) of 90 or above, meaning the colors you see under these lights are close to what you would see under direct sunlight at noon on a cloudless day, causing less strain to the eyes and brain. I prefer OttLite bulbs, but there are many others on the market. Use desk lamps rather than bright overhead lighting.

Allow children to wear brimmed caps indoors if that helps. The underside of the brim should be a dark color, such as gray, black or brown, to cut down on glare. Make sure children take frequent breaks rather than working through long stretches of time. When children tell you their eyes, head or stomach hurt from reading, believe them.

ADVOCATING FOR YOUR CHILD

Parents should advocate for their child at school. Ask the teacher to move your child as close to windows and natural lighting as possible. If wearing a hat with a brim to cut down on glare helps your child, ask that your child be allowed to wear one in the classroom. Ask that your child be given assignments on the colored paper that eases their stress when reading or on gray or beige rather than bright white. This is especially important during testing.

Once your child has been screened by a Certified Irlen Screener, have your child use the colored overlays at home and in school. If your child is willing to wear Irlen Spectral Filters (some are excited to, others resist), explain to your child's teacher why these are necessary and ask the teacher to explain to the other students how these special lenses help their classmate.

Another word of caution: If your child needs prescription eyeglasses altered so they work as Spectral Filters, be sure to find an eye doctor who is familiar with or open to learning about Irlen Syndrome. My community is fortunate to have an eye doctor who supports the work of the Irlen Institute and understands the importance of using Irlen Spectral Filters produced by the exacting standards of the Irlen Institute.

I once received a call from a woman who lives seventy-five miles from me. Her daughter had been tested by a Certified Irlen Diagnostician, but her two local eye doctors dismissed the efficacy of Irlen Spectral Filters, and even ridiculed the young woman. The mother decided to drive her daughter to the eye doctor in my community.

The Irlen Institute can help you find an Irlen Screener and Diagnostician in your community or one nearby. Screeners and Diagnosticians can then help you find the medical professionals in your community who can best serve your needs. They can also help you advocate for your child in the school they attend.

If your child does not need prescription lenses, then an Irlen Diagnostician can advise on the proper frames and lenses to be tinted by Irlen Institute technicians.

CONCLUSION

If your child struggles to read, and remedial intervention has not brought improvement, your child might have Irlen Syndrome, a visual processing problem. There are steps you can take immediately to help ease your child's symptoms, such are better lighting conditions and wearing a brimmed cap. Contacting a Certified Irlen Screener or Diagnostician through the Institutes website at irlen.com can bring you the answers and solutions you seek to help your child overcome the obstacles to fluid reading and better comprehension.

2

What Are Your Child's Symptoms?

Most children love to read. When words and numbers appear on the page as they should and learning progresses in a steady, predictable manner, finding adventure or information in a book is a pleasurable and rewarding endeavor. However, when reading causes headaches, stomachaches, or dizziness, children often give up and report they don't like reading. They may act out in class because of the embarrassment of being behind their classmates. They may think of themselves as, or be called, dumb and lazy. This is far from the truth, as those who suffer from Irlen Syndrome are usually as bright or brighter than average.

COMMON SYMPTOMS

Besides headaches, stomachaches, and dizziness, other symptoms of Irlen Syndrome can include migraines, a sensitivity to bright lights and glare, sleepiness, strain or fatigue, the need to take breaks or look away from the page when reading, a slow reading rate, inefficient reading, or lack of comprehension. It might manifest as poor depth perception with an inability to judge distances, poor sports performance, and difficulty taking escalators and stairs.

For many, the syndrome can cause the distortion of letters, words, numbers and symbols, especially with black ink on white paper. Irlen Syndrome can also cause difficulty when reading music. When writing, it may lead to trouble copying from one source to another, unequal letter size or spacing, writing up or down hill, and difficulty staying on a line.

DISTORTIONS

The distortions of the letters, words, numbers, or symbols may materialize in various ways. Distortions may include swirling or floating of words or words running off the page like bugs scurrying. Sometimes words bunch together or one line drops on top of another. Sometimes letters reverse themselves or turn upside down. Other times pages spark or crackle with distracting light flares. Numbers often misalign in their columns, and symbols may change so that a plus sign becomes a multiplication sign or vice versa. Sometimes words, numbers or symbols disappear altogether.

A self-aware teenaged boy I screened reported he preferred his school assignments on yellow paper, but didn't know why. When I had him read with a yellow overlay, his reading became smoother. I asked him to tell me what the page looked like when he read on white paper with black ink. He shrugged and said, "The words disappear." Without the overlay, he had to read one word at a time because any word he was not looking at directly would disappear. Instead of scanning several words ahead as proficient readers do, he had to move from one word to the next, causing his reading to be hesitant and choppy.

OBSERVING YOUR CHILD'S BEHAVIOR

Sometimes simple observations provide important clues to reveal that your child may be experiencing perception problems. Does your child rub his eyes or blink excessively after a few minutes of reading? Does she skip lines or lose her place? Does he complain of headaches or stomachaches? Does she bump into table edges or door knobs? Does he duck or step aside when a ball is thrown or kicked toward him?

The underlying issues of why your child is struggling to read may be caused by many factors. One of those factors, or even the only factor, could be Irlen Syndrome. The following questionnaire can help you to quickly identify if a problem with perception is causing your child to struggle with reading, writing, and sports performance.

QUESTIONNAIRE ABOUT SYMPTOMS

Observe your child's behavior or ask your child directly the following questions. Some children are aware of their symptoms. Some are not. As a parent, you will need to decide the best approach. Three yes answers indicate Irlen Syndrome may be present.

Reading Issues	YES	NO
1. Do bright lights hurt your eyes?	_____	_____
2. Does glare hurt your eyes?	_____	_____
3. Do your eyes ache when reading?	_____	_____
4. Do you blink a lot or squint when reading?	_____	_____
5. Do you get headaches when reading?	_____	_____
6. Do you move closer to or farther from the page?	_____	_____
7. Do you get tired quickly when reading?	_____	_____
8. Do you get stomachaches when reading?	_____	_____
9. Do you need to take breaks often when reading?	_____	_____
10. Do you get restless or fidgety when reading?	_____	_____
11. Do you skip words or lines when you read?	_____	_____
12. Do you need to reread words or sentences?	_____	_____
13. Do you lose your place when reading?	_____	_____
14. Do you complain about having to read?	_____	_____
15. Do these things get worse the longer you read?	_____	_____
TOTAL (Reading Issues)	_____	_____

The following questions are best answered by parents based on their observations.

Depth Perception Problems	YES	NO
16. Does your child have trouble catching a ball?	_____	_____
17. Does your child have trouble playing dodge ball or four-square?	_____	_____
18. Does your child have trouble hitting the ball in baseball or tennis?	_____	_____
19. Does your child knock items over often?	_____	_____
20. Does your child bump into table edges or door knobs?	_____	_____
TOTAL (Depth Perception Problems)	_____	_____

Other Areas to Observe	YES	NO
21. Does your child show fatigue from ordinary use of computer or television screens?	_____	_____
22. Does your child lack motivation or act discouraged?	_____	_____
23. Do your child's grades not reflect the amount of time spent on school work?	_____	_____
TOTAL (Other Areas)	_____	_____

Note: For a comprehensive questionnaire of more than 130 questions, please go to the Irlen Institute's website at irlen.com.

CONCLUSION

Parents are usually more aware of their child's symptoms and behaviors than the child is. However, if your child is self-aware, it is helpful to the child to be directly involved in the discovery of symptoms. Let your child know these symptoms may be caused by Irlen Syndrome and that there are ways to ease these symptoms so your child feels more comfortable. You may want to include your child's teacher in uncovering your child's symptoms because school is often a more stressful environment than home. Lighting conditions, schoolwork, and competitive situations could heighten your child's symptoms while in the classroom.

3

What Does Your Child See?

The earliest cooing sounds made by babies, "oo" and "ee," are the beginning of mastering complicated language skills. By six months a baby starts to babble or repeat sounds, such as "mamama" and "bababa," and by eight months they begin to link these sounds with objects, ideas, and thoughts. Beginning with cooing and babbling, to making short sounds, and in time words and phrases, babies learn to communicate with language. By the age of seven to eight most children can make all 44 sounds (phonemes) of the 26 letters in the English language.

LEARNING TO READ AND WRITE

The step from hearing and speaking these 44 sounds to being able to read and write is a major leap that starts with learning the sight of individual letters:

A B C D E F G H I J K L M N O P Q R S T U V W X Y Z

English speaking children usually do this by singing the ABC or alphabet song.

Next, children learn that each letter has one or more sounds. Except for H and W, all consonants have more than one sound. All vowels have both short and long sounds. Some letters have as many as seven sounds. This is a lot to learn. For children with Irlen Syndrome, it gets even more complicated.

To most children, the first letter of the alphabet looks like this: A

To children with Irlen Syndrome, letters may be distorted. For example, A may look like A.

These children are not aware of this. They think all people see the letter A the same way they do: A. They think everyone sees the alphabet the same too:

A B C D E F G H I J K L M N O P Q R S T U V W X Y Z

A reading disability at a time when the child is learning individual letters will most likely not be apparent. It may not even be apparent with simple words like CAT or DOG or FISH. The child learns that CAT, no matter how distorted, means this: .

READING TO LEARN

It is when children go from learning to read to reading to learn that the trouble truly begins. When confronted with an entire sentence or paragraph of distorted words, the challenges become severe:

Cats like to sit in the sun and take naps.

Imagine an entire paragraph or book of distorted words. This Chapter is meant as a guide for parents to use with a child who has any of the symptoms described in Chapter Two. The following illustrations of Gobblers distorting the words are used to underscore that this problem is not the child's fault. Like many disabilities it cannot be cured, but it can be overcome with the right tools and guidance.

TYPES OF DISTORTIONS

Pages 22–35 show examples of the distortions some people with Irlen Syndrome have with letters and words on the written page, especially with black ink on white paper. Pages 36 and 37 show examples of the distortions some people have with numbers. Many report just one distortion while others report dealing with several at once.

These pages will make it easier for those who do not have the syndrome: parents, teachers, siblings, friends, and classmates, to understand some of the challenges facing those who have the syndrome. For those with distortion symptoms, these pages will be even more confusing. Some children may report feeling nauseous or dizzy when looking at them. If this occurs, move through the pages that are causing a problem more quickly.

As you review the following pages with your child, notice if there is a recognition reaction, such as, "My words do that," or "My pages look like that." Not all Irlen Syndrome sufferers have distortions, and some only recognize their distortion(s) when viewed through the correct colored overlay(s), so a negative response does not rule out distortions being present. A Certified Screener or Diagnostician can uncover this symptom if it exists.

Sometimes Gobblers nibble the edges.

Once upon a time

Sometimes they chew through the middle.

there were three little pigs.

Sometimes they make letters vibrate.

The first little pig

Sometimes they make letters shake.
And sometimes they make letters jiggle.

met a man

Some Gobblers erase letters.

with a bundle of straw.

And some Gobblers wash them away.

The first little pig said

Gobblers can squish words together.

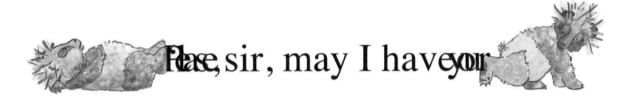

Please, sir, may I have your

And Gobblers can pull words apart.

straw to build a house!

Gobblers can make words run across the page.
If they do, then Word Gobblers are messing with you.

So the man gave the little pig his str
and the little pig built a house with it.
"No, no, no," said the second and
third little pigs. "Your house will not
be strong enough."

When sentences should look like this:

Once upon a time there were three little pigs.

Gobblers can make them look like this:

On ceupo nat ime the rewe reth ree litt lepigs.

When sentences should look like this:

The first little pig met a man with a bundle of straw. The first little pig said, "Please, sir, may I have your straw to build a house?" So the man gave the little pig his straw and the little pig built a house with it. "No, no, no," said the second and third little pigs. "Your house will not be strong enough."

Gobblers can make them look like this:

The first little pig **met** a man with a **bundle** of straw. The **little pig** said, "Please, **sir**, may I have your **straw** to build **a** house?" **So** the man gave **the** little pig his straw and **the** little pig **built** a house **with** it. "**No**, no, **no**," said the second **and** third **little** pigs. "Your **house will** not **be** strong enough."

When sentences should look like this:

The second little pig met a man with a bundle of sticks, and said, "Please, sir, may I have your sticks to build a house?" So the man gave the second little pig his sticks and the little pig built a house with them. "No, no, no," said the third little pig. "Your house will not be strong enough."

Gobblers can make them look like this:

The second little pig met a man with a bundle of sticks, and said, "Please, sir, may I have your sticks to build a house?" So the man gave the second little pig his sticks and the little pig built a house with them. "No, no, no," said the third little pig. "Your house will not be strong enough."

When sentences should look like this:

The third little pig met a man with a load of bricks and said, "Please, sir, may I have your bricks to build a house?" So the man gave the bricks to the little pig and the little pig built a house with them.

Gobblers can make them look like this:

The third little pig met a man with a load of bricks and said, "Please, sir, may I have your bricks to build a house?" So the man gave the bricks to the little pig and the little pig built a house with them.

When a page should look like this:

Along came a wolf. He knocked at the door of the first little pig, and said, "Little pig, little pig, let me come in." To which the pig answered: "No, no, by the hair of my chinny chin chin." The wolf answered, "Then I'll huff, and I'll puff, and I'll blow your straw house in." So he huffed, and he puffed, and he blew the house in. And the little pig ran to his brother's stick house. So the wolf knocked at the door of the second little pig, and said, "Little pigs, little pigs, let me come in." To which the pigs answered, "No, no, by the hair of our chinny chin chins." The wolf answered, "Then I'll huff, and I'll puff, and I'll blow your stick house in." So he huffed, and he puffed, and he blew the house in. And the two little pigs ran to their brother's brick house. The wolf knocked at the door of the third little pig, and said, "Little pigs, little pigs, let me come in." To which the pigs answered: "No, no, by the hair of our chinny chin chins." The wolf answered, "Then I'll huff, and I'll puff, and I'll blow your brick house in." So he huffed, and he puffed, and he huffed and he puffed, and he huffed and he puffed, but he could not blow the brick house in. The wolf went away with his tail between his legs. And the three little pigs lived happily ever after.

Gobblers can make it look like this:

Alongcamea wolf.Heknockedat thedoorofthefirstlittlepig. andsaid,"Littlepig,littlepig, letmecomein." Towhichthepig answered:"No,no,bythehair ofmychinnychinchin." Thewolfanswered, "Then I'll huff, andI'llpuff,and I'llblow yourstrawhousein."Sohe huffed,andhepuffed, andheblewthe housein.Andthelittle pigrantohisbrother'sstick house.Sothewolf knockedatthedoor ofthesecondlittlepig, and said,"Littlepigs,littlepigs, letmecomein." Towhichthepigs answered,"No,no,bythehair ofourchinnychinchins." Thewolfanswered, "Then I'llhuff, andI'llpuff,andI'llblowyour stickhousein."Sohe huffed,andhepuffed, andhe blewthehousein.Andthetwolittlepigs rantohisbrother'sbrick house.Heknockedatthe doorof the third little pig,andsaid,"Littlepigs, little pigs,letmecome in."Towhichthepigs answered: "No,no,bythehairofmychinnychin chins."Thewolfthen answered,"Then I'llhuff,andI'll puff,andI'llblowyourbrick housein."Sohehuffed,andhe puffed,andhe huffedandhe puffed,andhehuffedandhe puffed,buthecouldnotblowthe brickhouse in.Thewolf went away with his tail between his legs.Andthethreelittlepigslived happily ever after.

Or this:

Along came a wolf. He knocked at the door of the first little pig, and said, "Little pig, little pig,

let me come in." To which the pig answered, "No, no, by the hair of my chinny chin chin."

The wolf answered, "Then I'll huff, and I'll puff, and I'll blow your straw house in." So he

huffed, and he puffed, and he blew the house in. And the little pig ran to his brother's stick

house. So the wolf knocked at the door of the second little pig, and said, "Little pigs, little pigs,

let me come in." To which the pigs answered, "No, no, by the hair of our chinny chin chins."

The wolf answered, "Then I'll huff, and I'll puff, and I'll blow your stick house in." So he

huffed, and he puffed, and he blew the house in. And the two little pigs ran to their brother's

brick house. The wolf knocked at the door of the third little pig, and said, "Little pigs, little pigs,

let me come in." To which the pigs answered, "No, no, by the hair of our chinny chin chins."

The wolf answered, "Then I'll huff, and I'll puff, and I'll blow your brick house in." So he

huffed, and he puffed, and he huffed, and he puffed, and he huffed, and he puffed, but he could

not blow the brick house in. The wolf went away with his tail between his legs. And the three

little pigs lived happily ever after.

Or this:

Along came a wolf. He knocked at the door of the first *little pig*, and said, "Little pig, little pig, let me come in." To which the pig answered: "No, no, by the hair of my chinny chin chin." The wolf answered, "Then I'll huff, and I'll puff, and I'll blow your straw house in." So he huffed, and he *puffed, and* he blew the house in. And the little pig ran to his brother's stick house. So the wolf knocked at the door of the second little pig, and said, "Little pigs, little pigs, let me come in." To which the pigs answered, "No, no, by the hair of our chinny chin chins." The wolf answered, "Then I'll huff, and I'll puff, and I'll blow your stick house in." So he huffed, and he puffed, and he blew the house in. And the two little pigs ran to their brother's brick house. The wolf knocked at the door of the third little pig, and said, "Little pigs, little pigs, let me come in." To which the pigs answered: "No, no, by the hair of our chinny chin chins." The wolf answered, "Then I'll huff, and I'll puff, and I'll blow your brick house in." So he huffed, and he puffed, and he huffed and he puffed, and he huffed and he puffed, but he could not blow the brick house in. The wolf went away with his tail between his legs. And the three little pigs lived happily ever after.

Sometimes Gobblers make several things happen at once.
Gobblers are a nasty bunch.

Along came a wolf. He knocked at the door of the first little pig, and said:
"Little pig, little pig, let me come in."
To which the pig answered: "No, no, by the hair of my chinny chin chin."
The wolf answered: "Then I'll huff, and I'll puff, and I'll blow your straw house in."
So he huffed, and he puffed, and he blew the house in.
And the little pig ran to his brother's stick house.
So the wolf knocked at the door of the second little pig,
"Little pigs, little pigs, let me come in."
To which the pigs answered: "No, no, by the
The wolf answered: "Then I'll huff, and I'll puff, and I'll blow your stick house in."
So he huffed, and he puffed, and he puffed, and he blew the house in.
And the two little pigs ran to the third little pig's brick house.
He knocked at the door of the third little pig, and said:
"Little pigs, little pigs, let me come in."
To which the pigs answered: "No, no, by the hair of my chinny chin chins."
The wolf then answered, "Then I'll huff, and I'll puff, and I'll blow your brick house in."
So he huffed, and he puffed, and he huffed, and he puffed, and he huffed and he puffed.
But he could not blow the brick house in. The wolf went away with his tail between his legs.
And the three little pigs lived happily ever after.

Word Gobblers like to mess with numbers, too.
When rows and columns should look like this:

16943820657
37804315783
80325492917
49350661298
72804711590
59032149861
26184740309

Gobblers can make them look like this:

16943820657
37804315783
80325492917
49350661298
72804711590
59032149861
26184740309

Gobblers can change symbols, too,
or even make them disappear.

$8 + 2$ becomes 8×2

5×3 becomes $5 + 3$

$2 + 5$ becomes $2 \quad 5$

3×2 becomes $3 \quad 2$

CONCLUSION

Distortions come in many shapes. They are not limited to what is shown on these pages. Some Irlen sufferers see words swaying back and forth. Some try to catch them from flowing off the bottom of the page. Some see an entire page swirling. Some see flashes of light like sparklers in the night. Some see words growing larger while others recede. These are all due to the inability of the brain to properly process light waves. I have screened children and adults who run the spectrum from mild to severe. All have been helped with the knowledge of what the problem is and what tools are available to alleviate it.

4

Does the Color of the Paper Make Reading Easier?

A thirty-year-old woman who had been diagnosed with dyslexia when she was in sixth grade came to me for a screening. She was curious to see if she also had Irlen Syndrome. During her intake interview, she said when she was in sixth grade she'd been three years behind grade level in reading. After receiving remedial assistance and a specialized education plan, she'd caught up to grade level in less than a year.

I strongly suspected from this history that she did not have Irlen Syndrome. Those with both dyslexia and Irlen Syndrome have little positive response to remedial intervention unless the Irlen visual processing malfunction is alleviated first. After we finished with the task of narrowing down which colored overlay was most comfortable, she asked, "What if I still prefer black ink on white paper?"

I answered, "Along with being able to catch up on your grade level as a child and not having distortions or depth perception problems, I'd say you don't have Irlen Syndrome."

Those with Irlen Syndrome usually feel immediately more comfortable looking at the colored page that is correct for them. They often sigh or say things like, "That feels better."

HOW IMPORTANT IS THE COLOR OF THE PAPER?

For those who don't have Irlen Syndrome, the contrast between black ink and white paper helps the words stand out, making reading easier. But for those with the syndrome, black ink on white paper can cause problems because the contrast is too stark. The white background can overcome the black letters, making them fade or disappear or move on the page.

For some, white paper with black ink is physically disturbing, causing Irlen sufferers to blink excessively, rub their eyes, or look away from the page. For others, the white might glow or flash around the letters or shine like a neon sign, making it hard to concentrate and comprehend what is being read, and can cause headaches, dizziness, and fatigue.

The following exercises have been designed to help determine whether your child may be experiencing this specific problem. These exercises have been divided based on your child's age.

HOW TO USE THE FOLLOWING EXERCISES

In the next section, you will ask your child to read on white paper with black ink, then on colored paper. The exercise is fairly simple, so that it can be used by children who are not yet reading words—normally preschoolers and kindergarteners—but who do know the alphabet and numbers from 0 through 9. It can also be used by older children and even adults. The exercises are equal in difficulty but varied to avoid memorization.

Using the Exercises for Younger Children
[Eight or Younger]

The exercises are laid out on seven pages. The first page is white. Each of the six pages after white is a different color: beige, yellow, blue, pink, green or gray. The front side consists of three rows of letters and three rows of numbers. The back side consists of a short paragraph. Children eight or younger should skip reading the paragraphs.

Important: Please read the following instructions before moving on to the first exercise:

1. Determining Comfort Levels

Have your child look at the pages that contain the letters and numbers *without* reading them—that would be all the pages on the right. The first time through the pages you are looking for comfort level rather than accuracy. You will not ask the young child to look at the paragraph on the backside of these pages.

❑ As your child looks at these pages, ask if the letters and numbers are more comfortable to look at on the white page or on the colored page. You can flip from white to a colored page then back to white as you move through this section if that is helpful.

❑ It is important for your child to take a short rest between looking at each page by looking away for several seconds. This will give the eyes and brain time to adjust to each new color.

❑ After your child has looked at all the pages without reading, ask which color was the most comfortable. If your child has a hard time choosing, review the pages again. Be sure to emphasize that you want to know which color feels the most comfortable. Remember to have your child look away for several seconds between viewing each colored page. If you suspect your child is simply choosing a favorite color, say something like this: "I know that's your favorite color, and it can stay that way, but it's very important that you choose the color that feels the most comfortable when you look at the letters and numbers. Can you do that?"

2. Reading Letters and Numbers

Have your child read just the letters and numbers on the white page out loud. You will not be reading the paragraphs. Notice how your child sounds when reading. You are listening for ease and comfort, but also accuracy. Do not comment on your child's accuracy or mistakes, just move forward to the next step.

3. Determining the Best Color Background

Ask your child to read the letters and numbers on the most comfortable colored page out loud. Notice how your child sounds compared to reading the white page. Did it seem easier and smoother? Did your child make fewer mistakes or seem less stressed? If your child chose more than one colored page as comfortable, have them rest their eyes, then read from that page, too, and note the differences.

Once your child chooses a colored page that is the most comfortable, have the child take a rest for several seconds before moving on to the next exercise.

Using the Exercises for Older Children & Adults
[Nine and Up]

Follow the three steps above with the addition of having the older child or adult look at and then read the paragraphs on the backsides of the white and colored pages, if needed.

Older children may not show a problem when reading individual letters, but when given a paragraph to read, the discomfort level rises and the accuracy falls. Be sure to give them extra rest between reading the paragraphs.

If you can hear the child or adult reading the letters and numbers more smoothly on a specific color and they say that color is the most comfortable one then you do not need to have them read the paragraphs.

Read each letter out loud.

H B D C E M Y P T Z

L R Q F P A X V N K

U G J I R E W N O S

Read each number out loud.

5 9 8 4 2 2 7 0 1 6 3

3 6 9 0 5 9 2 4 8 1 7

8 1 5 9 6 7 4 3 0 2 9

Children nine and older should read the following paragraph out loud, if needed.

Why can birds fly? There are several reasons birds can fly. Their wings are the perfect shape for moving through the air. By pushing air under their wings and backwards, birds give themselves lift and forward motion. In addition, their wing and chest muscles are very strong for their size.

Read each letter out loud.

N M U H D E O R I A

W L F C A V Z P N S

Y H K X J Q R B T G

Read each number out loud.

7 3 4 2 5 1 8 0 7 9 6

4 1 8 7 9 2 4 6 0 5 3

6 2 0 5 8 3 1 7 9 4 8

Children nine and older: Read the following paragraph out loud, if needed.

What else helps birds fly? A bird's wingspan is in balance with its body size. The smallest bird, a bee hummingbird, is just two and a quarter inches long. Its wingspan is only one and a half inches. The largest bird, a wandering albatross, has an average body length of four feet and an average wingspan of ten feet.

Read each letter out loud.

G T U O P R I H N Q

X M Z J Y K L W C S

V A L T F I D B E P F

Read each number out loud.

6 4 3 9 0 1 7 2 8 3 5

4 1 6 7 2 5 1 8 3 9 0

7 3 6 2 9 4 0 8 1 5 2

Children nine and older: Read the following paragraph out loud, if needed.

Do a bird's lungs help it fly? Yes. Birds have large lungs for their size. This helps them take in a lot of air in a short time. The oxygen in air gives them energy. Birds also store air in their hollow bones. Air sacs are attached to the hollow areas and help take in oxygen while both inhaling and exhaling. This gives them extra energy needed for flight.

Read each letter out loud.

V N Q X I T Z J H K A

L U R S C N W B F D

M G L O E B P F Y P

Read each number out loud.

3 5 9 1 6 7 2 8 0 4

8 7 0 1 3 6 2 4 5 9

2 9 3 7 4 8 5 1 6 0

*Children nine and older: Read the following paragraph out loud,
if needed.*

Do hollow bones make a bird lighter? No. Researchers have
found that the hollow bones of birds are denser and heavier than
normal bones. They compared just the bones of a two-ounce
bird to just the bones of a two-ounce mouse. The bones of the
bird were heavier. The extra density makes the hollow bones
stronger and stiffer. This keeps them from easily breaking.

Read each letter out loud.

K A V B N L U K R Q

M Z F E S P W B R A

G O C Y X J I D P H T

Read each number out loud.

5 4 8 3 7 0 9 1 6 2

4 2 1 6 3 8 3 9 7 5

6 0 3 7 5 9 2 4 1 8

Children nine and older: Read the following paragraph out loud, if needed.

Do all birds have hollow bones? No. Diving birds such as penguins, loons, and puffins do not have hollow bones. This makes it easier to dive into and swim through water for food. Penguins cannot fly, but loons and puffins can. Soaring and migratory birds, such as robins, hawks and whooping cranes have many hollow bones, helping them stay aloft for many hours.

Read each letter out loud.

H X R D G Z D L U P

A R Q M F E Y J B K

W M V P T S I C O N

Read each number out loud.

6 2 3 8 0 5 4 7 9 1

8 3 1 6 4 2 7 3 0 5

7 9 5 4 0 7 1 6 9 2

Children nine and older: Read the following paragraph out loud,
if needed.

Do feathers help birds fly? Yes. Feathers are light weight and
can mesh together when a bird flaps its wings downward.
This makes a solid surface for pushing against the air. As
the bird moves upward, the feathers part, allowing the air
to pass through. The bird repeats this motion over and over
with the feathers meshing and parting with each stroke.

Read each letter out loud.

M O J H A S P R D B

Z V P T R E Y C I F X

N B W K I L U G Q E

Read each number out loud.

2 7 4 0 3 1 6 9 5 8

5 8 1 7 0 4 2 6 3 9

3 1 6 8 2 7 0 6 5 4

*Children nine and older: Read the following paragraph out loud,
if needed.*

Why do birds fly into windows? Birds do not know what
glass is. They see the sky and trees reflected in the glass and
think they have a clear path. If a male bird pecks or beats at
a window, it is because he sees his reflection and thinks it is
another male moving into his territory. This usually happens in
spring when he is looking for a mate and wants to build a nest.

CONCLUSION

If one of the colored pages makes reading easier or less stressful than reading on white paper, your child may have a light wave processing problem. Sometimes it takes a different shade of one of the colors provided here to make reading optimally easier or less stressful. For example, a child may prefer lavender to pink or orange to yellow, but the colors provided will narrow the field. A Certified Irlen Screener has hundreds of color combinations to choose from to determine if your child is likely to have Irlen Syndrome. A Certified Irlen Diagnostician also has hundreds of color combinations to choose from to determine if your child has Irlen Syndrome. In addition, a Diagnostician can provide thousands of color combinations to create the proper, scientifically-formulated Irlen Spectral Filters for your child.

5

It Is Not Your Child's Fault

Sadly, teasing and bullying can be a daily occurrence for children who have difficulty learning to read. They are often treated as if they are slow or dumb or lazy, when none of these things are true. Children are born with a natural curiosity about the world around them and the desire to learn, but as their world gets more complicated, obstacles appear for some.

It's a huge leap from manipulating blocks to holding a pencil; from finger painting to forming letters and numbers; from reading the twenty-six letters of the English alphabet to reading a book. Some children take this journey smoothly, one step at a time. Others, through no fault of their own, stumble again and again. They become discouraged and lose their motivation.

It is important for children to know there are solutions to the struggles they face. Some of the solutions are simple tools, such as using colored paper. Others are more complicated, such as wearing Irlen Spectral Filters. Most important, it is vital to their emotional well-being to know they have done nothing wrong. They are not at fault any more than someone who has an allergy to strawberries is at fault. It is also important that they realize they are not alone.

ASSURING YOUR CHILD

In this chapter, I hope to begin a conversation between you and your child. I have provided five important points designed to start a dialogue. Each of these pages are meant to be read out loud. The questions are meant to help open doors to a discussion of the things happening in your child's life. As you read through this chapter, you may find that there are many other questions you want to add to your discussion with your child. There is a page at the end of this chapter to jot down your notes. These areas of discussion include the following:

What Word Gobblers Do

This section is designed to discuss the possibility of physical symptoms your child may be experiencing along with their reading or learning problem, and will help to assure them that they are not the only ones.

Bullying

It is important to recognize that your child may be subject to name calling or bullying. Sometimes your child will not tell you about these incidents without your asking them directly. These questions should reveal whether or not this has occurred.

Lighting Up the Problem

This section will help your child become aware of the possibility that their difficulties are related to processing colors in the world around them.

Good Colors vs Bad Colors

Certain colors may be the source of a reading and/or learning issue. This section shows that bright lights and glare may make the problem worse.

Solving the Problem

Here you assure the child that there is a possible solution to help them overcome their difficulties.

The naughty Gobbler characters are meant to underscore the premise that your child is not at fault.

WHAT WORD GOBBLERS DO

To be read aloud by parent:

Word Gobblers can give you headaches and stomachaches.

They can make you squint and rub your eyes.

They can make you sleepy or antsy.

Do any of these things happen to you?

Do they happen to any of your sisters or brothers or cousins?

Do they happen to any of your friends or classmates?

If they do, you and they are not alone.

One in every six people in the world has Irlen Syndrome.

That's the same as ten in every sixty.

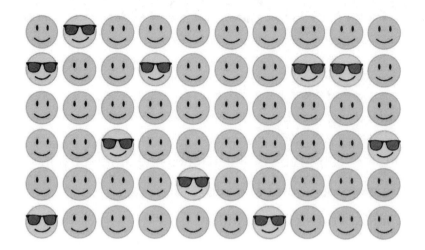

And the same as one hundred in six hundred.

BULLYING

Questions to ask your child:

1. Has anyone ever called you clumsy?

2. Has anyone ever called you lazy?

3. Has anyone ever called you slow?

4. Has anyone ever called you dumb or stupid?

You are **not** *any of these things.*

LIGHTING UP THE PROBLEM

If reading or writing is difficult,

or you have trouble judging distances,

or you have a sensitivity to bright lights and glare,

or you get headaches while reading or using a computer,

you may have a problem processing

specific colors of light.

GOOD COLORS VS BAD COLORS

Just like some people are allergic to certain foods,

such as wheat, milk, peanuts or strawberries,

because their bodies cannot process what those foods contain,

some brains cannot process certain colors of light

because of that color's wavelength.

People aren't clumsy, lazy, slow, dumb or stupid

just because they can't process certain foods.

And they aren't these things

just because they can't process certain light waves.

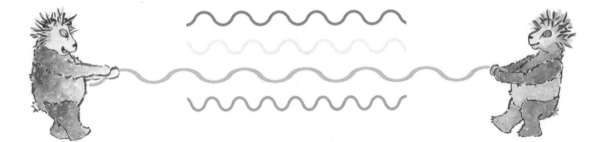

SOLVING THE PROBLEM

If colored paper, overlays, and Spectral Filters work for you,

they'll chase those Word Gobblers away.

And reading and writing and math

won't be so difficult

or stressful

anymore.

You may even find out

how much fun they

can be.

CONCLUSION

When children understand that their symptoms are caused by a physical problem that makes processing certain colors difficult or impossible for them, they realize they are not at fault. They realize they are not lazy or dumb. They realize they are not stupid or slow. They realize there is a reason why catching a ball or skipping rope or other types of sports are difficult for them.

When children learn there is a name for this condition—Irlen Syndrome—and that millions of people all over the world suffer from it just like they do, they realize they are not alone. And most importantly, they begin to feel better about themselves.

When they are given the tools to help overcome the problems caused by Irlen Syndrome, they achieve success and feelings of self-worth that can lead to even more success. Success as they themselves define it.

After observing your child's symptoms and talking to your child about the impact of those symptoms, use the following page to jot down notes of what you learn. These notes will be useful later when speaking to an Irlen Screener or Diagnostician to give them a more complete picture of your child's symptoms.

The notes will also be useful when speaking to your child's teachers and counselors about the difficulties your child is having, the reason for these difficulties, and the accommodations that are needed to help your child while in the classroom, such as using colored paper for assignments, sitting near a window for natural lighting, using a ruler or finger while reading, and wearing a hat with a brim.

NOTES

6

The Next Step

Now that you've read this book, observed your child's behaviors, answered the questionnaire, and worked through the tasks with your child, you'll need to decide if your child displays symptoms of Irlen Syndrome. If the answer is yes, it is key to your child's progress and success that you take the next step—finding a Certified Irlen Screener or Certified Diagnostician to do a thorough evaluation to determine its severity and the tools needed to calm the symptoms. The colored page samples in this book are limited, and while the questionnaire and exercises can help open the door to the possibility that a child has this condition, they cannot take the place of a trained Screener's or Diagnostician's expertise.

IRLEN SCREENING

To obtain the most accurate results, Certified Screeners and Diagnosticians are trained to use optimum lighting conditions, wall colors (white or beige), and even clothing colors (black or dark gray) when screening. Screeners have learned to observe a child's behavior during screening to see if they fit the profile and to ask questions in a manner that will elicit accurate answers.

They do not make judgments about a child's reading abilities. Their goals are to evaluate for Irlen Syndrome and advise on ways to ease the symptoms in an effort to increase reading efficiency and help a child move toward a more successful and comfortable life.

A Screener's toolkit contains questionnaires, including an Irlen Reading Perception Scale, exercises, a letter chart, task manual, and Irlen Overlays in ten colors. These colored overlays have been specially formulated by the Irlen Institute after years of research. Remember, it is never a good idea to buy overlays and simply spread them out and have a child "play" with them or pick a favorite. Using a favorite color rather than the correct color could do more harm than good. Also, a Screener is not limited to the initial ten colors. By expertly combining colored overlays, a Screener has hundreds of choices to help your child.

I'd like to see the day when every school has at least one teacher trained as a Certified Irlen Screener, and that every school aged child is screened. Until then, it is best to seek out a Screener or Diagnostician in your area who can meet the specific needs of each child.

CERTIFIED IRLEN DIAGNOSTICIAN

Certified Diagnosticians are trained to do the same evaluation as Certified Screeners, plus they are trained to test for Irlen Spectral Filters. If a Screener determines your child has Irlen Syndrome, the next step, and one I highly recommend, is to have your child tested by an Irlen Diagnostician for Irlen Spectral Filters which can be worn like glasses or contacts. A Diagnostician uses small, convex colored plastic disks to determine the best colors and in what order the colors should be placed to provide the greatest benefit. With more than fifty specially formulated colors, the Diagnostician has thousands of color combinations to offer. Some children need only one color, most need several, and a few need twenty or more. Each formula is individualized and specific to the user.

INDIVIDUALIZED SOLUTIONS

For those who are low on the spectrum of difficulty and who have no physical or behavioral symptoms, such as light sensitivity, headaches, stomachaches, depth perception problems, and sensory overload, colored overlays may be all that's needed to improve reading efficiency. However, for those in the mid to severe range with physical and behavioral symptoms, the brain needs relief for as many hours a day as possible, not just during time spent reading. Irlen Spectral Filters can provide that relief.

While screening a boy in sixth grade who was unable to read at a first grade level, I observed him looking away, rubbing his eyes, scratching his arms. His discomfort level was so high I had to keep the lights dim. He reported he had headaches almost every day and that white pages crackled with static like a television screen and that words were constantly jumping around on the page. Is there any wonder he couldn't read? I sent him home with three purple overlays to be used under various lighting conditions to help with the written page and a recommendation for Irlen Spectral Filters.

Whether your child falls on the spectrum at the low or severe end, help is needed. If you are interested in exploring Irlen Syndrome and the Irlen Method further or in finding a Certified Screener or Diagnostician near you, please go to irlen.com. The site contains in-depth scientific articles, videos of children reading with and without overlays or Spectral Filters, and both short and long self-administered questionnaires.

If you are interested in training to be a Certified Screener or Certified Diagnostician, please email the Institute at irlen.institute@verizon.net.

CONCLUSION

If your child displays symptoms of Irlen Syndrome, please take the next step by visiting the Irlen Institute's website at irlen.com to find a Certified Irlen Screener or Certified Irlen Diagnostician near you. Their expanded tool kits can help your child find the best solutions to their struggles with reading, writing, depth perception difficulties, physical symptoms, and behavioral problems.

Conclusion

In addition to children, I have screened many adults. Most adults have come to me because at some time in their lives, they suffered a brain concussion that led to symptoms of Irlen Syndrome. However, one adult client, a successful photographer and writer, was a fifty-year-old woman who'd not had any brain injuries, but suffered from a daily feeling of extreme stress. When I placed a peach colored overlay on top of a white sheet of paper with black lettering, she burst into sobs. I stayed calm, but couldn't help but wonder what I'd unleashed. After a few moments, she said, "Now my entire childhood makes sense." Within a month she was wearing Irlen Spectral Filters that had a golden hue.

My intention is that this handbook be used to intervene before a child grows into an adult, carrying the challenges of Irlen Syndrome into every aspect of life. I hope it can help parents discover what might be the cause of their child's difficulties with reading. There are many reasons children have reading problems, but if the problem is Irlen Syndrome, it must be dealt with first in order for specialized teaching methods to be effective. Once treated for Irlen Syndrome, a child is usually able to catch up to grade level within months, and the physical problems usually disappear or lessen.

Not all Irlen Syndrome sufferers have distortions like those in Chapter Three. Some have different types of distortions than those shown or they have eye strain, headaches, switching of letters and words, light sensitivity, fatigue, or other symptoms listed previously, but for those who have distortions, life is extra challenging.

Most people, including adults, think everyone sees the world and the printed page the way they do. They don't know they have distortions until they see a page through the correct colored overlay(s). They say things like, "Oh, that's what happens to me," or "Pages look like that to me." It's why children don't understand how classmates sitting next to them can read so easily when they cannot.

I meet adults every day who have struggled to read all their lives. Some have dealt with the physical stress of having Irlen Syndrome since childhood. Many choose not to read or to read only when necessary because of their employment or the need to follow written instructions. I hope this book will help children reach adulthood with the tools to make reading easier and more enjoyable, and to help them find whatever success they desire.

The researchers at the Irlen Institute continue to find other conditions that are eased by using Irlen Colored Overlays and Irlen Spectral Filters. These include ADHD, attention deficit/hyperactivity disorder, and autism. For those who seek additional information or a comprehensive list, the Irlen Institute can provide it at irlen.com. Click on Who We Can Help, then Medical Conditions.

Finally, I want to thank you for using this handbook to try to find answers to your child's reading difficulties and to bring relief from physical and emotional symptoms. I understand the heartache parents suffer when they see their child struggling. I hope this book will help you and your child along the path of success and fulfillment.

Glossary

ADHD. *See* Attention-Deficit/Hyperactivity Disorder.

Attention-Deficit/Hyperactivity Disorder. The disorder includes a combination of problems, including impulsive behavior. Symptoms can vary from person to person.

autism. Autism disorder impacts the nervous system and falls on a scale from mild to severe. Symptoms can include difficulty with communication and social interactions, obsessive interests, and repetitive behaviors.

decoding skills. Decoding involves taking apart the sounds in words. This ability is a key skill for learning to read. It helps children sound out unfamiliar words.

dyslexia. Dyslexia is a learning disorder that involves difficulty reading due to problems with a child's or adult's ability to decode.

Irlen Certified Screener. Screeners are trained to interview and administer a series of tests to determine if an individual is suffering from Irlen Syndrome.

Irlen Certified Diagnostician. Diagnosticians are trained to perform the same evaluation that Screeners perform to determine if someone is likely to have Irlen Syndrome. They are additionally trained in the exacting method of testing those with Irlen Syndrome in order to create each individual's specific formula for Irlen Spectral Filters.

Irlen Colored Overlays. These overlays are specially formulated colored plastic sheets used over black ink on white paper and on computer screens.

They ease the symptoms of those suffering from Irlen Syndrome by changing the high contrast black ink on white background to a color that the user's brain can more easily process.

Irlen Reading Perception Scale. This scale measures the level of perceptual difficulty and discomfort on a scale from 0 to 18 (severe) when looking at black patterns and text on a white background. This assessment is administered by an Irlen Screener or Diagnostician.

Irlen Spectral Filters. Spectral Filters are worn like eyeglasses. They are precision-tinted at the Irlen Institute for each individual. These lenses filter out the exact wavelengths of light creating perceptual difficulties and can improve problems with reading, headaches, migraines, dizziness, and depth perception.

Irlen Syndrome. Irlen Syndrome is a malfunction in the light wave or color processing center of the brain. It causes varied symptoms, one being difficulty with reading.

learning disabilities. These are any condition giving rise to difficulties in acquiring knowledge and skills at the level expected of those of the same age. The problems experienced vary from person to person, but may include difficulty learning new things, communication, managing money, personal care, reading and writing.

light waves. Light (waves) enables us to see the world around us. Some light waves are visible, while others are invisible. Light waves are measured in nanometers or nm. The human eye can see light waves from 390 nm to 700 nm. It is within this range of light waves that colors are produced that the human eye can see. These are the light waves that enter your eye and travel to your brain creating the image you see. Violet light is on the top of this spectrum while red light is on the bottom. Ultraviolet, as the name indicates, is above 700 nm and is invisible to the human eye.

Ottlite bulbs. These bulbs are color correcting, meaning the colors you see under these lights are close to what you would see under direct sunlight at noon on a cloudless day.

Other types of bulbs, such are incandescent and fluorescent, distort colors, causing problems for those who suffer from Irlen Syndrome. These can include headaches, migraines, dizziness, and distortions when reading.

phoneme. A unit of sound that distinguishes one word from another. English contains 19 vowel sounds and 25 consonant sounds for a total of 44 distinct sounds.

phonetic skills. The ability to sound out unfamiliar words by learning the basic five skills or rules needed to read the English language. These skills need to be mastered to become a good reader. These include:

1. When one consonant and nothing more follows the vowel, the vowel will be short, such as in the word *bat.*

2. When the vowel is followed by two consonants and nothing more, the vowel will be short, such as *call.*

3. When a vowel stands alone, it will be long, such as *I*

4. When a word ends with a silent E the first vowel will be long, such as *make.*

5. When vowels are next to each other, the second vowel is silent and the first vowel is long, such as *boat.*

sight vocabulary. A set of words that a child can immediately recognize without use of decoding strategies. Many sight words cannot be sounded out, so mastery of these words is one key component to success in reading. There are over two hundred of these words. Examples include: *enough, right, sign, laugh, again, know, once, said,* and *where.*

spectrum. Any scale used to classify or measure something in terms of its position on a scale between two extremes or opposite points. Autism is classified this way, as is Irlen Syndrome.

Resources

BOOKS

Calkins, Lucy, with Lydia Bellino. *Raising Lifelong Learners: A Parent's Guide.* Cambridge, MA: Perseus Books, 1997.

This book explains the importance of what and how a child learns at home. It shows ways to turn a home into a rich learning environment and offers chapters on the usual classroom subjects of reading, writing, and math, but also on play and chores. The information in this book can supplement learning in a traditional school setting or offer guidance to those who homeschool.

Irlen, Helen L. *Certified Irlen Screener's Information Handbook.* Long Beach, CA: Irlen Institute International Headquarters, 2018.

Continuously updated Screener's manual with training materials, questionnaires, intake forms, and research information.

Irlen, Helen L. *The Irlen Revolution: How a Simple Method Can Change the Lives of Children and Adults with LD, AD/HD, TBI, Dyslexia, Autism, Headaches, Medical Conditions, and Much More.* Garden City Park, NY: Square One Publishers, 2010.

An updated version of Helen Irlen's first book, *The Irlen Revolution* contains the latest information and discoveries involving perceptual processing problems and how all aspects of life can be affected, from reading and writing to depth perception to medical and psychological conditions.

Irlen, Helen L. *Reading by the Numbers: Overcoming Dyslexia and Other Reading Disabilities through the Irlen Method.* New York, NY: Perigee Books, 1991, 2005.

This second edition explains the science behind learning disabilities caused by a perceptual processing problem within the brain. Through the use of brain-imaging techniques that were not available when the book was first published in 1991, the reader will learn why one in six people worldwide suffer from a condition now called Irlen Syndrome. The book offers steps that can be taken to assess if that condition applies and steps that can be taken to ease or eliminate the symptoms.

Irlen, Helen L. *Sports Concussions and Getting Back in the Game of Life: A solution for Concussion Symptoms including Headaches, Light Sensitivity, Poor Academic Performance, Anxiety and Others.* Long Beach, CA: Helen Irlen, 2015.

Sports and combat related brain injuries often produce long term, debilitating physical symptoms, including headaches, dizziness, nausea, light sensitivity, memory loss, blurred vision, and irritability. The same methods that ease the symptoms of Irlen Syndrome, a light processing problem within the brain can also relieve the symptoms of these type of injuries.

Jordan, Dale R. *Overcoming Dyslexia in Children, Adolescents, and Adults.* Austin, TX: PRO-ED., Inc., 1996.

Starting with the history of dyslexia, this book takes the reader through the twentieth century workplace, visual and auditory dyslexia, and how individuals with this learning disability can achieve success.

WEBSITES

Irlen Institute
Website: www.irlen.com

This website offers the most up to date information and research on Irlen Syndrome. The website includes videos of children reading with and without colored overlays and with and without Irlen Spectral Filters. Questionnaires are provided to self-assess whether one may have Irlen Syndrome. The viewer can also use the site to find local Certified Irlen Screeners or Diagnosticians.

The Reading Well—a virtual well of dyslexia resources
Website: Dyslexia-Reading-Well.com

Their mission is to help parents and teachers understand dyslexia and connect to resources. They provide a well-defined section on phonemes—the smallest units of speech sound that convey a unique meaning.

About the Author

Catherine Matthias is a Certified Irlen Syndrome Screener. She is also the published author of six early reader picture books published in English and Spanish. Her two nonfiction books were part of a career series titled *I Can Be a Police Officer* and *I Can Be a Computer Operator.* Catherine's fiction titles are *Over-Under, Out the Door,* and the popular *I Love Cats* and *Too Many Balloons.*

Her love of children's books began when she worked in a preschool in Cheltenham, Pennsylvania during her mid-twenties. *The Word Gobblers* is a natural extension of her Irlen Screening work, her picture book writing, and her desire to see all children enjoy reading. After living for many years in Portland and Lake Oswego, Oregon, Catherine now lives with her husband, Stewart Jones, in rural Joseph, Oregon with a view of the beautiful Wallowa Mountains. She can be contacted through her writer's website: www.CatherineMatthias.com.

Index

The Irlen Revolution

A Guide to Changing Your Perception and Your Life

Helen Irlen

The widely accepted notion that everyone sees the exact same thing when looking at the objects around them is wrong. For instance, while one person can pick up a printed page and read it with ease, another may be frustrated by words and letters that appear to move and jump around. Fortunately, there is a noninvasive, effective solution—the Irlen Method. After three decades of revolutionizing the treatment of reading issues with the use of colored filters, Helen Irlen has turned her attention to children and adults who suffer from light sensitivity, headaches, attention deficit disorder, learning disabilities, dyslexia, and a host of other visual perception-related conditions. Here, finally, is hope for everyone who has been misdiagnosed and needs real help for a real problem.

The book begins by telling Helen's journey, focusing on her work with struggling readers and detailing how she eventually discovered the Irlen Method. A detailed description of an Irlen Screening is provided, including strategies you can try at home. Finally, the author discusses the individual issues and disabilities that can get in the way of learning—what they are and how the Irlen Method can be used to treat them effectively. Each chapter deals with a different disability and includes questionnaires that you can use to become your own detective and find the root cause of the difficulty. Rounding out the book is an extensive appendix, which explores an array of other possible causes of attention, concentration, performance, and academic problems; provides recommendations for treatment; and offers helpful resources.

Problems in processing visual information can cause physical symptoms and fragmented vision that affect attention, concentration, and performance. Thankfully, there is an easy, cost-effective solution—the Irlen Method.

About the Author

Helen Irlen, MA, BCPC, LMFT, a graduate of Cornell University, is a credentialed school psychologist, licensed therapist, adult learning disability specialist, and expert in the area of perceptual processing disorders. While working with adults with learning disabilities, Irlen made a discovery that resulted in marked improvement in her students' reading abilities. Today, there are numerous affiliated Irlen Testing Centers worldwide that use the Irlen Method to overcome a wide range of perceptual-processing problems.

$17.95 US • 244 pages • 6 x 9-inch quality paperback • ISBN 978-0-7570-0236-6

**For more information about our books,
visit our website at www.squareonepublishers.com**